# The Execution of Mary Queen of Scots

By Sir Robert Wingfield of Upton

Being an eyewitness account held in the
Bute Archives at Mount Stuart

## FOREWORD BY ANTONIA FRASER

Edited with an introduction and postscript
by Andrew McLean

MOUNT STUART
2007

Published by The Mount Stuart Trust
Mount Stuart, Isle of Bute, Scotland PA20 9LR

First published in 2007
Copyright © The Bute Archives, Mount Stuart Trust and Andrew McLean (ed.) 2007.
Copyright © Foreword Antonia Fraser 2007.

Copyright © photographs The Bute Archives 2007.
Photography by Keith Hunter and Andrew McLean.

A CIP catalogue record for this book is available from the British Library.

ISBN 978-0-9544748-5-0

Designed by Paul Barrett.
Design, editorial and production in association with
Book Production Consultants Ltd, 25–27 High Street, Chesterton,
Cambridge CB4 1ND, United Kingdom.
Printed and bound in the United Kingdom by The Burlington Press,
Cambridge, United Kingdom.

**Front cover:** Engraved book illustration depicting the execution of Mary Queen of Scots, the first dramatic depiction to appear in print. Taken from Richard (Rowlands) Verstegan, *Theatrum crudelitatum haereticorum nostri temporis*, Antwerp, 1587.

**Back cover:** Portrait of Mary Queen of Scots which was based on the 'Blairs Memorial Portrait' commissioned by Elizabeth Curle who had accompanied Mary at her execution.

# CONTENTS

# FOREWORD

## Antonia Fraser

It is over four hundred years since the execution of Mary Queen of Scots at Fotheringhay, and over forty years since I personally visited Fotheringhay for the first time. Yet it is still impossible to read an eyewitness account of that scene at the Northamptonshire Castle without emotion. Various contemporary narratives have been printed, including that of Queen Mary's physician Bourgoing, who was with her for several months before her death and present at the last. Here the important first-hand narrative, published for the first time, comes from the opposite point of view. The writer, Sir Robert Wingfield, was reporting to his uncle Lord Burghley, Elizabeth's powerful minister – and Mary's enemy.

Yes, there is remarkable coherence in the picture which emerges. Here is a middle-aged woman, her fatal beauty long gone, captive for nearly nineteen years, who nevertheless has the courage and determination to direct her own death – direct it spiritually, that is, since she can have no control over the actual circumstances. Wingfield, by giving the full text which the Protestant Dean of Peterborough intended to deliver to the Catholic Queen in her last moments, makes this additionally clear. Mary intends to die not as a traitor, but as a witness to her Catholic faith. I still treasure the dried thistle I picked at Fotheringhay from those known as 'Queen Mary's Tears': tears not shed in vain.

# INTRODUCTION

## Andrew McLean, Bute Family Archivist

Shortly after 9 a.m. on the morning of 8 February 1587, within the Great Hall of the Castle of Fotheringhay, Northamptonshire, two strokes of an executioner's axe finally extinguished the life of Mary Stuart, Queen of Scots, Dowager Queen of France, and, to her supporters, rightful Queen of England. The tragic outcome of Mary's life and death has often been told, and yet the grizzly circumstances of her end – after many years held as the captive of her cousin, Elizabeth Tudor, Queen of England – continue to exert a morbid fascination more than four centuries after the fatal strokes were administered. Within a year of her death printed tracts and pamphlets relating the sensational events which had taken place at Fotheringhay – several illustrated with engravings depicting Mary's final moments – began to appear across Europe; and in the centuries since Mary's life and death have become the subject of books, plays and even Hollywood movies (one of the earliest films ever made was *The Execution of Mary Stuart*, released in 1895). Today, the cult of Mary remains as strong as ever, and unquestionably her story is the best known of any Scot in history.

Yet for all the imagined glamour surrounding Mary's tragic tale, the real story needs no embellishing. Indeed, if one delves deep and examines the original sources it is clear that, as just one episode in an improbable life full of romance, intrigue, violence and treachery, the execution itself is a story rich in drama and remarkable incident. Queen Mary's carefully stage-managed outfit, her astonishing fortitude in facing up to certain death, the executioner failing with his first strike, and Mary sneaking her little dog into the execution chamber hidden under her skirts are no imaginings of a Hollywood scriptwriter but actual documented events.

Of all the accounts of the execution, the most important is arguably that prepared by Sir Robert Wingfield of Upton in Northamptonshire (*c.*1558–1609), a key witness to this drama who would probably have stood no more than 10 feet from Mary when the decisive blows fell. This account was commissioned at the highest level of English government, being produced, as Wingfield's dedication

Frontispiece to *Execution Oder Todt Marien Stuarts Königinnen aus Schotlandt gewesenen Königinnen zu Franckreich...Anno 1587*, Johan Francken, Magdeburg, 1588.

makes clear, at the command of his uncle William Cecil, Lord Burghley, Elizabeth's chief minister and the man credited as being most responsible for bringing about Mary's demise. Throughout her life Mary had many foes, but none as tenacious (or as obsessed) as Burghley, the man above all others who remained her sworn enemy to the bitter and violent end. Completed three days after the event, Wingfield's surprisingly objective account is a remarkably powerful, immediate and dramatic piece of reportage.

Wingfield, son of Robert Wingfield of Upton (d. 1580) and Elizabeth, daughter of Richard Cecil of Little Burghley and sister of Lord Burghley, was a wealthy and respected Northamptonshire gentleman and served for many years as Member of Parliament for Stamford. As well as observing the execution, he also went on to play a prominent role in the burial of Mary's body at Peterborough Cathedral on 1 August 1587 (nearly six months after her death), when he acted as one of the eight men or 'bannerolls' who carried heraldic banners depicting the coats of arms of Mary's ancestors during the funeral procession.

This version of Wingfield's account – here published in full for the first time – is held in the Bute Archives at Mount Stuart on the Isle of Bute, one of the most important archival collections in Scotland. Acquired by John Crichton-Stuart, 4th Marquess of Bute (1881–1947) in 1930, the account was formerly in his library at 5 Charlotte Square in Edinburgh, before being moved to Mount Stuart during the 1950s. Since its purchase the account

Portrait of Mary Queen of Scots which was based on the 'Blairs Memorial Portrait' commissioned by Elizabeth Curle who had accompanied Mary at her execution.

has been viewed by only a select few and its existence was largely forgotten until its rediscovery during the reorganisation of the library and archive collections at Mount Stuart in the 1990s.

Contained within a thin octavo volume comprising thirty-eight pages of manuscript, the Bute execution account is written on paper bound within limp vellum covers. There are various other manuscript versions of Wingfield's account known, each one differing in varying degrees from the others, but none is as lengthy or as detailed as the Bute manuscript.

One version, Landsdowne MS. 51, is held in the British Library and was published in the 1820s.[1] Extending to some four pages, this is a far less detailed version than the Bute copy, but it is endorsed in Lord Burghley's own hand:

'8. Febru[ary] 1586. The man[n]er of y[e] Q[ueen] of Scotts deth at fodry[n]ghay wr[itten] by Ro. Wy.' Although unquestionably a copy that came into Burghley's possession, it is impossible to tell if it is the earliest surviving example of Wingfield's account (it does not appear to be written in his hand), although it is certainly a good deal shorter and consequently lacks much of the drama of the Bute manuscript.

Other known variants are held in the Surrey History Centre (Loseley Collection, LM/1921) and the Bodleian Library (Tanner MS. 78), and both of these were published in two separate works in the late nineteenth century.[2] These were probably produced shortly after the execution, the former being a copy belonging to the puritanical Sir William More of Loseley (1520–1600), a friend of both Lord Burghley and Queen Elizabeth, who had a deep personal interest in Mary's fate, having served on several English govern-

John Crichton-Stuart, 4th Marquess of Bute, who acquired the manuscript in 1930.

Pages from Robert Wingfield's account of the execution of Mary Queen of Scots, 1587. The pages shown here include a description of the beheading itself.

mental committees set up to address the problems and issues arising from her imprisonment in England.

Finally, this brings us to the Bute manuscript and another copy in the British Library, from the celebrated collection of Sir Robert Cotton (d. 1631).[3] The Bute and Cotton versions are remarkably similar and offer a more comprehensive description than the other known copies. These appear to have been draft texts prepared for publication as a tract, a popular means in the days before daily newspapers of spreading news of significant events or of getting a political or religious message across (often illegally). Each has features that are lacking in at least one or all of the other known copies, namely: a dedication to Lord Burghley; a detailed description of Mary's appearance on the day of her execution; and a full account of the sermonising of the rather unappealing Richard Fletcher, Dean of Peterborough, who bullies, harangues and rebukes Mary and her religion (apparently this is not all it seems, and was only added to the text on Fletcher's insistence as he had failed to deliver this intended speech on the day of the execution, after a dramatic altercation with Mary in which the Queen emerged triumphant).[4]

Although there are possible similarities in the handwriting of both the Bute and Cotton manuscripts, it is difficult to be certain that the same person has copied them as there are a number of differences in how certain letters are written and various words spelt. Confusingly, the Bute manuscript may be in the hand of two different scribes as the handwriting changes for some (though not all) of the quotations from direct speech (such as the Dean of Peterborough's prayer).[5] Nevertheless, it appears that the Bute version – neater and with more standardised spelling – is the second and final draft of the text intended for a publisher and, perhaps significantly, both have a blank space waiting to be filled with the words Mary spoke in French on the scaffold.[6]

Aside from variations in the spelling of certain words and minor grammatical and structural differences, the most significant textual distinction between the Bute and Cotton manuscripts is that – tantalisingly – in the Bute version there appears (in a different hand) one amendment written in the margin. Here the word 'sanctification' is given as a correction to 'satisfaction' in the draft text. This is a potentially crucial clue as 'satisfaction' appears uncorrected in the Cotton manuscript, suggesting that the Bute version is the final draft of Wingfield's complete text and is probably the one intended for the printer's press. Intriguingly the word 'sanctification' appears in the speech by the Dean of Peterborough that is believed to have been added to the account, as we have seen, at a later date on the Dean's insistence. This, and the fact that the Dean's speech appears to be in a different hand, do raise currently unanswerable questions about the manuscript, and one wonders who was responsible for editing the account – did the Dean and Lord Burghley attempt to edit it more favourably to serve their own ends? This one word means that the Bute manuscript is a more complete version than the Cotton manuscript and thus – it can be strongly argued – survives as the most important and detailed known copy of the various versions of Wingfield's account.[7]

In the event, the text was not printed and why it was withheld from going to press remains unclear, although it is possible that the English government – continuing to wage a propaganda war against Mary even after her death, and

Piece of embroidery believed to have been worked on by Mary Queen of Scots during her captivity in England.

Proclamation issued by Queen Elizabeth announcing the sentence of guilt passed against Mary for her alleged role in a plot to murder Elizabeth and place Mary on the throne, 4 December 1586.

believing that her reputation would only have been enhanced by the strength of her character, which shines forth from the pages – was afraid of widely publicising the execution through the publication of Wingfield's writings. Moreover, after Mary's death the apparently grief-stricken Queen Elizabeth – deeply aware of the potential problems which might arise from government-induced regicide – attempted to shift the blame for the carrying out of the execution (or 'a miserable accident', as she called it in a letter to Mary's son, James VI of Scotland[8]) on to others. The subject would remain a delicate one for many years afterwards.

What became of the manuscript after it was written is unknown until the nineteenth century, when it was in the possession of George Folliott who built up an important (if little-known) collection of manuscripts, paintings and books that he kept in his house at Vicars Cross, on the outskirts of Chester. Folliott died in 1851, and the bulk of his collections were eventually sold in a series of sales held on the instruction of his daughter and grandson at Sotheby's in May 1930, at which the London dealer Charles J. Sawyer purchased the execution account for £30. Lord Bute acquired the manuscript from Sawyer in November of that year at the considerably higher price of £230.

Bute, himself directly descended from the Royal House of Stuart, was an avid collector of manuscripts and artefacts relating to the family. He built up a small but important collection of material relating to Mary Queen of Scots. It includes not only Wingfield's execution account, but also samples of needlework worked by her during her captivity, contemporary printed tracts on Mary's life and death, and a printed copy of the proclamation issued by Elizabeth I on 4 December 1586 announcing the sentence passed against Mary for her alleged role in the Babington plot (a poorly thought-out scheme instigated by Anthony Babington, a young Catholic gentleman, with the intention of murdering Elizabeth and placing Mary on the English throne in her place[9]). Lord Bute was also one of the main contributors to the cost of acquiring Mary's last letter (written at Fotheringhay on the morning of the execution) for the nation in 1918.[10]

As we have seen, it appears likely that the Bute version of Wingfield's account was intended for publication. Perhaps because of wariness about publicising Mary still further (for even in death she remained a dangerous figure to the English government), this was not progressed, but now – over four centuries later – the full text, adapted into modern English, appears in print for the first time.

# THE EXECUTION OF MARY QUEEN OF SCOTS

## A note on the text

The text has been rendered into modern English to make it as accessible to as wide a variety of readers as possible. Modern punctuation and capitalisation have also been added where none exists in the original manuscript. Words added in square brackets do not appear in the original text. Wingfield's original structure of paragraphs has been retained. All historical illustrations are taken from items in the Bute Collection.

## *Dramatis personae*

An alphabetical list of persons mentioned in the text.

| | |
|---|---|
| Andrews, Thomas | Sheriff of Northamptonshire. The manuscript mistakenly states Norfolk. |
| Beale, Robert | Clerk of the Privy Council. |
| Burghley, Lord | Sir William Cecil, Lord Burghley and Lord High Treasurer of England (1520–98). He was chief minister to Elizabeth I and the prime mover in forcing through Mary's execution. Burghley commissioned this account from his nephew Robert Wingfield of Upton. |
| Curle | Elizabeth Curle, sister of Gilbert Curle, Mary's secretary. She was one of Mary's female attendants and was present at the execution. |
| Drury, Sir Drew | Drury was assistant to Mary's gaoler Sir Amyas Paulet and her joint custodian from late 1586 until her death. |
| Fletcher, Dr Richard | Dean of Peterborough and later Bishop of London. He was the father of John Fletcher, the dramatist, who was a friend and collaborator of Shakespeare. |

| | |
|---|---|
| Kent, Earl of | Henry Gray, 16th Earl of Kent, was one of the two commissioners of Elizabeth I at Mary's trial and execution. |
| Mary Queen of Scots | Mary succeeded her father James V soon after her birth in 1542. She spent much of her childhood in France, where she was betrothed to – and later married – the French dauphin, Francis. She was Queen of France for a short period until her husband's premature death in 1560. On returning to Scotland, she faced a country riven by religious and political disputes. Two further marriages, both highly controversial, destabilised Mary's position further. Forced to abdicate in 1567, she escaped captivity and fled to England in 1568. There she was held as Queen Elizabeth's prisoner until her execution in 1587. |
| Melville, Andrew | Mary's loyal Steward, mistakenly named 'Melvyn' in each of the surviving versions of Wingfield's account. He afterwards returned to Scotland and married Jane Kennedy, one of Mary's closest companions during her final years. |
| Melvyn | See Melville, Andrew. |
| Paulet, Sir Amyas | Mary's custodian from 1585 until her death. |
| R.W. | See Wingfield, Robert. |
| Shrewsbury, Earl of | George Talbot, 6th Earl of Shrewsbury, had been custodian of Mary Queen of Scots from 1569 to 1584 and was Elizabeth's other commissioner at the execution. |
| Wingfield, Robert | The author of this account, he was Burghley's nephew and served as MP for Stamford for many years. He had a prominent role in Mary's funeral at Peterborough Cathedral in August 1587. Knighted in 1603 he died at Upton, Northamptonshire, in 1609. He is buried in the impressive Church of St Kyneburgha, Castor, not far from Upton. |

*A* True Narration of the Execution of Mary late Queen of Scotland within the Castle of Fotheringhay the eighth day of February Anno Domini one thousand five hundred [and] Eighty six.[11]

### And

Directed to the Right Honourable Sir William Cecil, Knight, Lord Burghley and Lord High Treasurer of England.

### By R.W.

The Epistle Dedicatory to the Right Honourable Sir William Cecil, Knight, Lord Burghley [and] Lord High Treasurer of England.

It may please your good Lordship to be advertised, that according as your honour gave me command, I have here set down in writing the true narration and manner of the execution of Mary, the late Queen of Scotland, the eighth day of February last past, in the Great Hall within the Castle of Fotheringhay, together with relation of all such speeches and actions spoken and done by the said Scottish Queen or any others and all circumstances and proceedings concerning the same from and after the delivery of the said Queen to Thomas Andrews, Esquire, High Sheriff for her Majesty's county of Norfolk, unto the end of the said execution as follows.

The Execution of Mary late Queen of Scotland.

It being certified the sixth of February[12] last to the said Queen by the Right Honourable the Earl of Kent, the Earl of Shrewsbury, and also by Sir Amyas Paulet and Sir Drew Drury, her governors, that she was to prepare herself to die [on] the eighth day of February then next coming, she seemed not to be in any terror for ought, that appeared by any her outward gestures, or behaviour of her, then marvelling she should die, but rather with smiling cheer and pleasant countenance digested and accepted the said ordination of preparation to her (as she said) unexpected execution, saying that her death should be welcome unto her, seeing that her Majesty[13] was so resolved and that her soul were so far unworthy [of] the fruition of the joy of heaven for ever, whose body would not in this world be content to endure the stroke of the execution for a moment and that spoken she wept bitterly and became silent.

The said eighth day of February being come and the time and place appointed for the execution as aforesaid of the said Queen of Scots, being of stature tall, of body corpulent, round shouldered, her face fat and broad, double chinned, and hazel eyes, her borrowed hair auburn,[14] her attire was this:

On her head she had a dressing of lawne[15] edged with bone lace, a pomander chain and an Agnus Dei about her neck, a crucifix in her hand, a pair of beads at her girdle with a golden cross at the end of them, a veil of lawne fastened to her cowl bowed out with wire and edged round about with bone lace, her gown was of black satin printed with a train and long sleeves to the ground, sewed with acorn buttons of jet trimmed with pearl and short sleeves of black satin cut, with a pair of sleeves of purple velvet whole under them.

Her kirtle whole, of figured black satin, her petticoat upper body, unlaced in the back, of crimson satin,[16] and her petticoat skirt of crimson velvet, her shoes of Spanish leather with the rough side outward, a pair of silk garters coloured green, her stockings worsted coloured watched clocked with silver and edged in the top with silver, and next [to] her legs a pair of Jersey hose white.

This Queen thus apparelled, in a kind of joy without any desire of deferring of matters or time, departed her chamber and very willingly bended her steps towards the place of execution, being gently supported out of her said chamber into an entry next [to] the said Great Hall by two of Sir Amyas Paulet's chief gentlemen, Mr Andrews the High Sheriff going before her; in which entry the honourable the Earl of Kent and the Earl of Shrewsbury, commissioners appointed by her Majesty for her said execution, together with the two governors of her person Sir Amyas Paulet and Sir Drew Drury and divers other knights and gentlemen of good account, did meet her, where they found one of the said Queen's servants named Melvyn[17] kneeling on his knees to the said Queen his mistress, wringing his hands and shedding tears, used then and there these words unto her:

'Ah, Madame, unhappy me, what man on earth was ever before the messenger of such important sorrow and heaviness as I shall be, when I shall report that my good and gracious Queen and Mistress is beheaded in England.'

This said tears prevented him of further speaking, whereupon the said Queen, pouring out her dying tears, thus answered him:

'My good servant, cease to lament for thou has cause rather to joy than to mourn for now shalt thou see Mary Stuart's troubles receive their long expected end and determination, for know,' said she, 'good servant, all the world is but vanity and subject still to more sorrows that a whole ocean of tears can bewail, but I pray thee,' said she, 'carry this message from me that I do die a true woman to my religion and like a true woman of Scotland and France, but God forgive them,' said she, 'that have long desired mine end and thirsted for my blood, as the hart doth for the water brooks.

'Oh God,' said she, 'thou that art the author of truth and truth itself knows the inner chamber of my thoughts how that I was ever willing that England and Scotland should be united together. Well,' said she, 'commend me to my son and tell him that I have not done anything prejudicial to the State and Kingdom of Scotland.' And so resolving herself again into tears [she] said: 'Good Melvyn, farewell.' And with weeping eyes, her cheeks all besprinkled with tears as they were, [she] kissed him, saying once again: 'Good Melvyn,' and, 'Pray for thy mistress and Queen.' And then she turned herself to the Lords and told them that she had certain requests to make unto them. One was for a sum of money which she said Sir Amyas Paulet knew of to be paid to one Curle her servant. Next that her poor servants might have and enjoy that with quietness which she had given them by her Will and Testament, and that they might be favourably entreated and to send them safely unto their countries, 'and this to do my very good Lords, I do command you.'

Answer was made to this effect by Sir Amyas Paulet: 'I am not forgetful of the money your grace doth speak of, and therefore,' said he, 'your grace shall not need to rest in suspense of the not performing [of] your request.'

And then, she said, there rested yet one request which she would make unto the Lords and that was this – that it would please them to permit her poor distressed servants to be present about her at her death, that their eyes might behold and their hearts be witnesses how patiently their Queen and mistress should endure her execution that, thereby, they might be able to relate, when they come into their countries, that she died a true constant Catholic to her religion.

Then the Earl of Kent answered thus: 'Madame, that which you have desired cannot be conveniently granted, for if it should, it were to be feared least some of them, with speeches or other behaviour, would both be grievous to your grace, and troublesome and unpleasing to us and our company whereof we have seen experience, for if such an access should be allowed they would not stick to put some superstitious trumpery in practice, and it were but in dipping their handkerchief in your grace's blood, whereof were very unfit for us to give allowance.'[18]

'My Lord,' said the Queen of Scots, 'I will give my word, although it be but dead, that they shall not deserve blame in any [of] the actions you have named but, alas, poor souls, it would do them good to bid their mistress farewell.

'And I hope,' said she, 'further to see, the Earl of Kent, your mistress' – meaning her Majesty[19] – 'being a maiden Queen will vouchsafe in regard of womanhood that I shall have some of my own people about me at my death.

'And I know,' said she, 'her Majesty hath not given any such straight commission but that you might grant me a request of far greater courtesy than this, if I were a woman of far meaner calling than the Queen of Scots.' And then perceiving she could not obtain her request without some difficulty, of mere grief [she] burst into tears saying:

'I am cousin to your Queen and descended from the blood Royal of King Henry the Seventh and a married Queen of France and an anointed Queen of Scotland.'[20]

At which time, upon great consultation betwixt the two Earls and others in commission, it was permitted that she should have some of her servants about her as before she had instantly desired and entreated, and withal did desire her to make choice of half a dozen of her best beloved men and women, and then of her men she chose Melvyn, her apothecary, her surgeon, and one other old man besides, and of her women she chose [those] that did use to lie in her chamber.[21]

After this the said Queen, being supported by Sir Amyas Paulet's gentlemen as aforesaid and Melvyn carrying up her train, being accompanied too by the Earl of Kent's gentleman and the Sheriff going before her as aforesaid, passed out of the centre into the Hall within the said Castle of Fotheringhay before mentioned, and with an unappalled countenance stepped up to the scaffold in the Hall, then and there made for her death, being two foot high and twelve foot broad with rails round about, hanged and covered with black, with a low stool, a long fair cushion and a block covered also with black.

Then having the stool brought [to] her, she sat down. On the right hand of her there stood the Earl of Kent and the Earl of Shrewsbury, and on the left hand Mr Andrews the Sheriff, and opposite before her stood the two executioners, and round about the scaffold stood gentlemen and others.

Then silence being made, the Queen's Majesty's Commission for her execution was read openly by Mr Beale, clerk of the council. Which done the people with loud voice said, 'God Save the Queen.' During the reading of which said Commission the said Queen was very silent, listening unto it with so careless regard as if it had not concerned her at all. Nay rather with so merry and cheerful a countenance as if it had been a pardon from her Majesty and withal used such a strangeness in her words and deeds as if she had never known any of the assembly nor had been anything seen in the English language.

Then Mr Doctor Fletcher, Dean of Peterborough, standing directly before her without the rails [and] bending his body with great reverence, uttered this exhortation following:

'Madam, the Queen's most excellent Majesty[22] whom God long preserve to reign over us, having (notwithstanding this preparation for the execution of justice, justly to be done upon you for your many trespasses against her sacred person, state and government) a tender care over your soul, which presently departing out of your body must either in the true faith of Christ live for ever, doth by Jesus Christ offer unto you the comfortable promises of Almighty God, to all penitent believing Christians, wherein I beseech your grace even in the bowels of Jesus Christ to consider these things shortly:

'First, your estate past and transitory glory;

'Secondly, your condition present of life to mortality;

'Thirdly, your estate to come either to everlasting happiness or perpetual infelicity.

'For the first let me speak with David the King. Forget, Madame, yourself, your own people, and your father's house. Forget your natural birth, your regal and princely dignity, so shall the King of Kings have pleasure in your spiritual beauty. Make all things as dust and seeing that you may be found of God not having your own righteousness, which is defiled and unclean, but the righteousness of God by faith in Jesus Christ upon and in all that believe that you may know him, whom to know is life everlasting, and the virtue of his resurrection, to raise you up at the last day to life everlasting and the fellowship of his passion that if you suffer with him, you may be glorified by him and the conformity of his death, that by the partaking and communion whereof you may die to sin and live again to righteousness.

'And that in your former course, Madame, you be not judged of the Lord, repent you truly of your former sins and wickedness and justify the justice now to be executed upon you, and justify her Majesty's faithfulness and favour towards you. At all times have a lively faith in Christ our Lord and Saviour, so shall [you] be rightly prepared unto death.

'If your offences, Madame, were as many as the sands upon the sea and as red and bloody as scarlet, yet the fellowship of the Lord, the grace and mercy of God the Father, through the passions and obedience of Jesus Christ by the sanctification[23] of God, the Holy Ghost, shall purify and make them as white as snow and shall cast them into the bottom of the sea and remember them no more.

'The special means to attain this forgiveness of sins is neither in man, nor by man, but by faith in whom we being justified have peace with God and spiritual security.

'Secondly, consider, I beseech your grace, your present condition of life to mortality, your going from hence to be no more seen, your departure into a land where all things are forgotten, your entry into a house of clay, where worms shall be your sisters and rottenness and corruption your father. As Job speaketh, where the tree falls there it must lie, whether it be towards the south of life and blessedness, or towards the north of death and dolefulness, now is the time of your rising to God, or your falling into utter darkness where shall be weeping, wailing and

Series of four illustrations from Adam Blackwood's, *La Mort de la Royne d'Ecosse, Dovairiere de France ...* Paris, 1589. These show Mary being read the death warrant whilst in her chamber at Fotheringhay, her praying in her chamber with her distraught servants prior to her execution (her pet dog — which plays a memorable role in the execution — is also shown), her being led to her execution and the execution itself showing Mary's severed neck from the first misdirected blow of the executioner's axe.

gnashing of teeth, hereafter there is no time of reconciliation nor place of satisfaction where life is gotten, where it is lost. And therefore this day, Madame, yea this house, if you will hear God's voice, harden not your heart for the hand of death is over your head, and the axe is put to the root of the tree, the throne of the great Judge of heaven is laid open and the books of all your life are spread wide and the particular sentence of judgement is at hand.

'But if you fly to the throne of grace with boldness in Christ, only meritorious obedience, and apply it to your soul with the hand of true faith, your Christ shall be your life and your death shall be your advantage, and nothing else but an entry into everlasting glory, and this your mortality shall in a moment put on immortality.

'Madame, now Madame, even now doth God Almighty open unto you heavenly kingdoms in comparison whereof all earthly principalities are as darkness and as the shadow of death.

'Shut not up, therefore, this passage by the hardening of your heart, and grieve not the spirit of God which may seal your hope to a day of redemption.

'Thirdly, and lastly, I pray your grace weigh with yourself the time and state to come either to rise in the day of the Lord, unto the resurrection of life and to hear that joyful and blessed (Venite), come you blessed of my father, or the resurrection of condemnation replete with sorrow and grief (Ite), go you cursed into everlasting fire, there to stand on God's right hand, as a sheep of his pasture, or on his left hand, as a goat prepared unto vengeance, either to be gathered as wheat unto his barn or to be cast out as chaff into a furnace of unquenchable fire.[24]

'Blessed are the dead which die in the Lord, in the Lord shall you die, if in true faith you desire to be dissolved and to be with Christ, with Christ shall you be if you make Christ your only sacrifice for your sins and ransom for your redemption.

'Ah, Madame, trust not to the desires which God's words doth not warrant, which is the true touchstone and clear light to lead and guide our feet into the way of peace.

'Jesus Christ yesterday and today and the same forever, and in him are all the promises of God fulfilled as the scripture testifies: that through faith in his blood we and all God's Church shall receive remission of sins.

'In him all the saints called in the day of their trouble, and have been heard and delivered. In him have they all trusted and were never confounded. All other cisterns, Madame, are broken and cannot hold the water of everlasting life.

'The name of the Lord is a strong tower, whereunto the righteous fly and be saved, and there from, Madame, that you may so glorify him in this your last passage, that you may be glorified of him for ever, I most humbly beseech your grace for the tender mercy of God to join with us present in prayer to the throne of his grace, that we may rejoice and you be converted, and that God may turn his loving kindness and countenance and grant you his grace.'

In uttering of which exhortation the said Queen, three or four times, said unto him:

'Trouble not yourself, Mr Dean, not me, for know that I am settled in the ancient Catholic and Roman religion, and in defence thereof by God's grace I mean to spend my blood.'

Then said Mr Dean, 'Madame, change your opinion and repent you of your former wickedness and settle you upon this ground that only in Christ Jesus you hope to be saved.'

Then she answered and said with great earnestness:

'Good Mr Dean, trouble not yourself any more about this matter for know I was born in this religion and am resolved to die in this religion.'

Then said the two Earls (when they saw how far uncomfortable she was to the hearing of Mr Dean's good exhortation): 'Madame, we will pray for your grace that if it stand with God's Will you may have your heart enlightened with the true knowledge of God and his word and so die therein.'

Then answered the said Queen: 'My Lords, if you will pray with me I will even from my heart thank you and think myself greatly favoured by yours, but to join with you in prayer, my Lords, after your manner, who are not of one and the self-same religion with me, it were a sin and I will not.'

Then the Lords called for Mr Dean again and had him say on, or speak that he thought good, whereupon the said Mr Dean kneeling upon the scaffold stairs began this prayer following:

'O most gracious and merciful father, who according to the multitude of thy mercies doest put away the sins of them that truly repent, that thou remembers them no more. Open, we beseech thee, thy eyes of mercy and behold this person appointed unto death whose eyes of understanding and spiritual light, albeit thou has hitherto shut up, that the glorious beams of favour in Jesus Christ do not shine unto her but is possessed with great blindness and ignorance of heavenly things, a certain token of thy heavy displeasure if thy mercy do not triumph against thy judgement. Yet impute not unto her, O Lord God, we beseech thee, these her offences which separate her from thy mercy and if it may stand with thine everlasting purpose and good pleasure, O Lord, grant unto us, we beseech thee, thy humble servants this mercy which is about thy throne, that the eyes of her may be lightened and converted unto thee, and grant her also if it be thy blessed Will the heavenly comfort of thy Holy Spirit that she may taste and see how gracious the Lord is. Thou hast no pleasure, good Lord, in the death of a sinner and no man shall praise thy name in the pit. Renew in her, we most humbly beseech thy Majesty, whatsoever is wrought in her either by her own frailty or by the malice of the ghostly enemy; visit her, O Lord, if it be thy good pleasure, as thou didst your offender at your side of the Cross with this consolation, 'This day shalt thou be with me in paradise'. Say unto her soul as thou did unto thy servant David, "I am thy Salvation."

'Grant these mercies, O Lord, unto us thy servants to the increase of thy kingdom and glory at this time. And further preserve, we most humbly beseech thee, in long and honourable peace and safety, Elizabeth our most natural sovereign, Lady and Queen. Let them be ashamed and confounded, O Lord, that seek her soul, let them be turned back and put to confusion that wish her evil and strengthen still, O Lord, we pray thee, thy hand and balance of Justice amongst us by her gracious government; so shall we now and ever rest under thy faithfulness in truth, as under a shield and buckler, bless thy name and magnify thy mercy which lives and reigns one most gracious God for ever and ever Amen. Amen.'

All the assembly, saving the said Queen [and] her servants, said the prayer after Mr Dean.

During the saying of which prayer, the Queen herself sat upon a stool, having about her neck an Agnus Dei, in one of her hands a crucifix, at her girdle a pair of beads with a golden cross at the end of them, with a Latin book of vain prayers in her other hand.

Thus furnished with her superstitious trumpery without any regard had to that which Mr Dean said, [she] began very justly, with tears and a loud voice, to pray in Latin, and in the midst of her praying, by reason of overmuch weeping and mourning as it seemed, she began to slide off her stool at which time, kneeling again, said diverse other prayers in Latin and so she left praying before Mr Dean.

When Mr Dean had done she prayed in English for Christ's afflicted Church and for an end of her troubles, for her son and for the Queen's Majesty, and desired God that she might prosper and serve God aright. That spoken, she said she hoped to be saved by and in the blood of Jesus Christ at the foot of whose crucifix, holding that up which she had in her hand, she would shed her blood.

Then said the Earl of Kent, 'Madame, I beseech you settle Jesus Christ in your heart as you did before and leave the addition of these popish trumperies to themselves.'

She seemed little or nothing at all to regard the good counsel of the said Earl of Kent but went forward with her prayers and in the conclusion thereof, in English, desired God that it would please him to avert his wrath from this island and that he would give unto it grace and forgiveness of sins.

Then she said that she forgave all her enemies with all her heart who had long sought her blood and desired God to convert them to the truth. This done, she desired all saints to make intercession for her to the saviour of the world, Jesus Christ.

Then she began to kiss her crucifix and to cross herself, saying these words, 'Even as thy arms, O Jesus Christ, were spread here upon the Cross, so receive me, I beseech thee, into thy arms of mercy and forgive me all my sins,' and so ended.

Then the two executioners[25] kneeled down and desired her to forgive them her death. She answered, 'I forgive you with all my heart for I hope this death shall give an end to all my troubles.'

Then they with her two women began to disrobe her and then she laid her crucifix upon the stool. One of her executioners took from her neck the Agnus Dei, and then she began to lay hold of it, saying she would give it to one of her women and withal told the executioner that he should have money for it.[26]

Then she suffered him with her two women to take off her chain of pomander beads and of all her other apparel and that with a kind of gladness and smiling she began to make her self unready, putting off a pair of sleeves with her own hands (which the two executioners before had rudely been taking off) and that with such speed as if she longed to have been gone out of the world.

During all these actions of disrobing of the said Queen, she never altered her countenance, but smiling as it were said she never had such grooms before to make her unready, nor ever did put off her clothes before such a company.

At length she being untired [and] unapparelled of much and so much of her attire and apparel as was convenient, saving her petticoat and kirtle, her two women looking upon her burst out into a very great and pitiful shrieking and when their crying began to decline they crossed themselves and prayed in Latin.

Then said the Queen, turning herself to them and seeing them in such a mournful and lamentable plight, embraced them and said these words in French *Ne crie vous j'ai promis pour vous.*[27] And so [she] crossed and kissed them and bade them pray for her and not to be mournful. 'For,' said she, 'this day I trust shall your mistress's troubles end.' Then with a smiling countenance she turned herself to her menservants, Melvyn and the rest, standing upon a bench near unto the scaffold, who were sometimes weeping and sometime crying out aloud and continually crossing themselves [and] prayed in Latin, and the said Queen thus turned unto them, did herself likewise cross them, and bade them farewell and prayed them to pray for her even unto the last hour. This done, one of her women, having a Corpus Christi cloth,[28] lapped it up three cornerwise and kissed it and put it over the face of her Majesty and pinned it fast upon the cowl of her head.

Then the two women mournfully departed from her and then the said Queen kneeled down upon the cushion at which time and hour resolutely and without any token of fear she spoke aloud this Psalm in Latin: *In te Domine, confido ne confundar in eternum.*[29]

Then, groping for the block, she laid down her head, putting her chin over the block with both her hands, which holding them still had been cut off, had they not been espied.

Then she laid herself upon the block most quietly and stretching out her arms and legs cried out: *In manus tuas Domine*[30] three or four times, and at the last, while one of the executioners held her slightly with one of his hands, the other gave two strokes with an axe before he cut off her head, yet left a little gristle behind, at which time she made very small noise and stirred not any part of herself from the place where she lay.

Then the executioner that cut off her head lifted it up and bade, 'God save the Queen.' Then her dressing of lawne fell off from her head, which appeared as grey as if she had been three score and ten years old, polled very short, her face being in a moment so much altered from the form which she had when she was alive as few could remember her by her dead face. Her lips stirred up and down almost a quarter of an hour after her head was cut off.[31]

Then said Mr Dean, 'So perish all the Queen's enemies.'

And after the Earl of Kent came to the dead body and standing over it with a loud voice said likewise: 'Such an end happen to all the Queen's and the Gospel's enemies.'

Then one of the executioners, plucking off her garters, espied her little dog which was crept under her clothes, which would not be gotten forth but with force, and afterwards would not depart from her dead corpse but came and lay between her head and shoulders, a thing diligently noted.

The same dog being imbued with her blood was carried away and washed as all things else were that had any blood on them. The executioners were sent away with money for their fees, not having any thing that belonged unto her.[32]

Afterwards everyone was commanded forth of the Hall saving the Sheriff and his men, who carried her up into a great chamber made ready for the surgeons to embalm her and [she] was embalmed.

And thus I hope (my very good Lord) I have certified your honour of all actions, matters and circumstances as did proceed from her or any others at her death, wherein I dare promise unto your good Lordship if not in some better or worse words than were spoken somewhat I am mistaken in matters I have not any whit offended.

Howbeit I will not so justify my duty herein but that many things might well have been omitted as not worthy noting, yet because it is your Lordship's fault to desire to know all and, so I having certified all, it is an offence pardonable. So resting at your honour's further commandment I take my leave this XIth of February Anno 1586.[33]

Your honour's, in all humble service to be commanded, R.W.

Finis.

# Postscript

Unlike on 8 February 1587, when there was unseasonably fine weather at Fotheringhay – a sign, the Dean of Peterborough later remarked, that heaven looked on Mary's execution with favour – the corresponding date in 2007, exactly 420 years after Mary's horrific end, witnessed the heaviest fall of snow in Northamptonshire for many years. Perhaps wishing to shut itself away from the world on this, the anniversary of the single most notorious event in its history, Fotheringhay was inaccessible and isolated, the road thickly white and unclear. The irony of this is profound, for here was the site of a significant royal castle, the birthplace of one controversial monarch, Richard III, and the place of death of another, but today Fotheringhay is so overlooked that the authorities do not even bother to clear the road into the village. Even if the curious visitor had managed to make it through the snow, there would have been little to see of the once

View looking across the River Nene to the site of Fotheringhay Castle. Fotheringhay Church appears in the background.

The site of Fotheringhay Castle today showing the motte on the left. The flat ground to the right was where the hall in which Mary was beheaded stood.

impressive fortress – described by one observer as 'fair and mightily strong' – save for a large mound of earth (the remnants of the motte), one hefty chunk of masonry and the partially filled-in remains of the outer and inner moats. How very different it was 420 years earlier, when Fotheringhay was the scene of one of the most dramatic events in European history. So how did this once important centre of the power of the English monarchy come to be like this?

Today Fotheringhay is a picturesque village with a handsome church (once mooted as a burial place for Mary herself), which survives as an especially fine example of medieval English parish-church architecture. Here, with a slow majesty, the River Nene gracefully winds its way past the spartan site, once Mary's final place of captivity, in which her vital organs were apparently buried at the time her body was embalmed. It was here, for six months after her execution, that Mary's body remained securely imprisoned within the Castle complex, while the fretful authorities, concerned not to create a place of pilgrimage, argued over the

Photograph of the west front of Peterborough Cathedral by George Washington Wilson, c.1875.

best fate for her corpse. Mary's loyal servants, many of them constant companions during large stretches of her captivity and for whom the Castle had long been home, continued to be imprisoned within it, until finally being allowed their freedom in August 1587. With their release the full story of Mary's beheading would at last be told. Fotheringhay Castle, perhaps believed to be a cursed place, fell into ruins, its structure robbed,[34] and today it has largely vanished from view. It is certainly true to state that Mary died at Fotheringhay, and it is perhaps also true to say that Fotheringhay died with her.

Eventually, Queen Elizabeth ordered that Mary should be accorded a state funeral and that this should take place within the magnificent surroundings of Peterborough Cathedral (already home to the body of one Queen, Henry VIII's first wife Katherine of Aragon, who died in 1536). Mary's body was spirited out of Fotheringhay on a funeral carriage draped in black velvet and richly decorated with the Royal Arms of Scotland in the middle of the night of 30 July and silently processed by torchlight to Peterborough, where it arrived at around 2 a.m. on the morning of 31 July, the day before the funeral.

Dedicated to St Peter and, appropriately, Scotland's patron saint, Andrew, Peterborough witnessed a ceremony that reflected Mary's Scottish heritage to some degree. The arms of her Scottish (as well as her French and English) ancestors were carried during the funeral procession – one of them, as mentioned in

Engraved view of the tomb of Mary Queen of Scots in Westminster Abbey from George Chalmers, *The Life of Mary, Queen of Scots*, 2 vols., London, 1818.

*South view of the Monument of Mary Queen of Scots with aisle of Henry 7 Chapel Westminster Abbey.*

Engraved portrait of Mary Queen of Scots with caption referring to her being mother to King James VI and I from William Stranguage's *The Historie of the Life and Death of Mary Stuart Queene of Scotland*, London, 1624.

the introduction, being carried by Robert Wingfield himself. However, that was about all that Mary would have approved of, for no Scot – save her loyal Steward Andrew Melville and Barbara Mowbray, wife of her secretary Gilbert Curle – and none of her relations was present; and the ceremony, carried out by the Bishop of Lincoln and her execution-day adversary, the Dean of Peterborough, was a Protestant one.[35]

The heavy lead-lined coffin, said to be in excess of 9 hundredweight, was manoeuvred into the Cathedral with some difficulty and Mary's body was eventually interred in a tomb prepared by the remarkable sexton, one Robert Scarlett, better known as 'Old Scarlett', for he was now in his ninety-first year. Scarlett, noted as being of 'sturdy limb' and 'mighty voice', had also buried Katherine of Aragon and was said to have dug graves for the population of Peterborough 'twice over'. Fittingly, on his own death seven years after Mary's funeral, Scarlett himself was buried inside the Cathedral and his grave marker can still be seen; above it hangs his portrait, in which he stands beside a pick and shovel, the tools of his trade. Below the portrait sits a poetic memorial tablet that extols his virtues and notes his principal claim to posterity: 'He had interred two Queens within this place.'

While Scarlett's memorials are today a noted attraction in Peterborough Cathedral, Mary's body is no longer there.[36] In 1612 her son James VI of Scotland, by then James I of England also, had her mortal remains removed to a majestic tomb in the Lady Chapel in Westminster Abbey, where she lies close to her Tudor great-grandfather Henry VII. On the opposite side of the chapel – in a less impressive tomb – lies one of Henry's granddaughters, Mary's old adversary Elizabeth I herself. And here lies the great irony of Mary's demise and Elizabeth's hollow victory, for Elizabeth, the 'Virgin Queen', died childless and with her death in 1603 the direct Tudor line was extinguished. It was Mary's son, James, who succeeded Elizabeth as England's first Stuart monarch, and it is from Mary that all subsequent monarchs, right down to the present Queen, may claim direct descent, whereas none may from Elizabeth. In life Mary adopted the motto 'In my end is my beginning', a prophecy that became unquestionably true in death.

And what of Robert Wingfield, the man to whom we owe this dramatic account of Mary's final hours? He was an ambitious man and because of the good service he did for his uncle, the powerful Lord Burghley, at the execution he may have expected to have been rewarded for his loyalty by protection and prefer-ment. His attempts to win favour with Elizabeth were, however, to be dashed. Although he served for many years as Member of Parliament for Stamford, he failed to achieve any position in government, causing him to lament that he was 'no way able to deserve a favourable look, much less a good turn'. After Elizabeth's death he sought to win over the new monarch, but although James knighted him in 1603, Wingfield, despite additional attempts to curry favour, continued to be overlooked. However, with Burghley's death in 1598 Wingfield had probably lost his greatest chance of preferment, and he himself died at Upton on 24 August 1609, still vainly hoping to 'deserve the … favour' of a monarch whose mother's death he had so memorably recorded twenty-two years previously.

A. Mc., 11 February 2007, the 420th anniversary of Wingfield's completing his account of the execution of Mary Queen of Scots.

# ENDNOTES

1.  Henry Ellis, *Original Letters Illustrative of English History*, 2nd series, vol. III, London, 1827, pp. 112–118.
2.  See Charles Dack, *The Trial, Execution and Death of Mary Queen of Scots*, Northampton and London, 1889, pp. 1–17; and The Hon. Mrs Maxwell-Scott, *The Tragedy of Fotheringay*, London, 1895, pp. 249–256.
3.  Bute Archives, MQS/1 (ex Bute MS. 324); British Library, Cotton Collection, Caligula, C IX, ff. 637–647 – this has been printed in A. Francis Steuart, *Trial of Mary Queen of Scots*, Edinburgh and London, 1923, pp. 173–184. Steuart mistakenly gives Wingfield's Christian name as Richard.
4.  Fletcher's failure to deliver this 'attempted sermon' has been described by John Guy as the 'greatest *faux pas* of his career'; see his book *'My Heart is My Own': The Life of Mary Queen of Scots*, London, 2004, pp. 5–6.
5.  Who the scribe or scribes were is unknown but comparing the handwriting here with known letters written by Robert Wingfield demonstrates that the handwriting is not his (for one possible exception see endnote 7 below).
6.  See p. 28.
7.  Although the main body of the text is clearly not in Wingfield's hand, there are some stylistic similarities with Wingfield's handwriting, as there are in the way in which the word 'sanctification' is written in the margin.
8.  Letter dated 14 February 1587, reprinted in William K. Boyd (ed.), *Calendar of State Papers Relating to Scotland and Mary, Queen of Scots 1547–1603*, Glasgow, 1915, no. 280, p. 285.
9.  The proclamation was formerly in the Loseley Collection, and probably belonged to Sir William More, mentioned earlier.
10. National Library of Scotland, Adv.MS.54.1.1.
11. By modern calendar reckoning 1587 – at this time the English New Year began on 25 March, 1 January only becoming officially recognised as the start of a new year in 1752 (Scotland had adopted 1 January as New Year's Day in 1600).
12. This is an error. Mary was informed on the eve of the execution, 7 February.
13. i.e. Queen Elizabeth.
14. Borrowed hair – in other words, she wore a wig.
15. Lawne: a fine linen resembling cambric.
16. Crimson would have been deliberately chosen as it is the liturgical colour of martyrdom.
17. Actually Andrew Melville, Mary's Steward.
18. Here 'unfit' has been taken as the meaning, from the original word 'unmeete' in the manuscript. Kent was concerned that a handkerchief dipped in Mary's blood could be used as a symbol of martyrdom.
19. i.e. Queen Elizabeth.
20. Henry VII's daughter Margaret Tudor had married King James IV of Scotland in 1503, and the son of this marriage, later James V, was Mary's father.

21. These being: Andrew Melville, her Steward; Jacques Gervais, her surgeon; Dominique Bourgoing, her physician; Didier Syflart, her porter; and her closest female companions, Jane Kennedy and Elizabeth Curle.

22. It was at this stage that the Dean apparently blundered over the speech which follows. See the introduction, p. 10.

23. 'Sanctification' has been added in the margin, indicating that it should replace the word 'satisfaction' in the text.

24. This passage concerns the Final Judgement as presented in Matthew 25 offering the choice to come (Venite) into Heaven or go (Ite) into everlasting damnation.

25. The principal executioner's surname was Bull; he was the headsman of the Tower of London and was said to be the finest executioner in England. Curiously, his Christian name cannot be confirmed although it was probably Simon.

26. It was one of the perks of the executioner's job that he could take a memento from the belongings of his victim.

27. As at this point a blank space appears in both the Bute and Cotton manuscripts, the words here given – which may be translated as 'Do not cry but rejoice' – are taken from other known versions of Wingfield's account.

28. A veil of silk or lace used to cover the receptacle in which the host is reserved.

29. Taken from Psalm 30, verse 2: *In te Domine speravi non confundar in aeternum in iustia tua salva me* (In thee, O Lord, have I hoped, let me never be confounded: deliver me in thy justice). Roman Catholic translation.

30. Psalm 30, verse 6, an invocation for a happy death: *In manus tuas, Domine, commendo spiritum meum* (Into thy hands, O Lord, I commend my spirit). Roman Catholic translation.

31. The severed nerve endings continued to move, giving the appearance that she was still reciting *In manus tuas domine*.

32. The authorities were concerned that any objects belonging to Mary, or drops of her blood, could be removed from the scene and used as symbols of martyrdom – even in death Mary remained a threat to the English Crown.

33. In modern calendar reckoning 11 February 1587– see endnote 11.

34. A romantic myth developed that in a fit of anger James VI and I ordered the Castle to be demolished. In fact it fell into ruin through neglect, and local builders and landowners robbed it of its materials. The Great Hall itself was rebuilt by the antiquary Sir Robert Cotton in his house at Connington (itself now demolished), while the staircase down which Mary is said to have walked towards her death (as well as windows out of which she may have glimpsed the outside world for the last time) were rebuilt during the 1630s in the Talbot Hotel in nearby Oundle, where they can still be seen. A carved heraldic lion from the Castle is now in the porch of Fotheringhay Church.

35. Other Scots from Mary's household staff at Fotheringhay attended the procession but refused to enter the Cathedral for a Protestant service.

36. Fittingly, the site of her burial is today guarded by the Saltire and Lion Rampant.

# ACKNOWLEDGEMENTS AND FURTHER READING

## Acknowledgements

The editor would like to thank the following for assisting in the production of this book: the Bodleian Library, Oxford; the British Library, London; William Burke, Rector of St Kyneburgha's Church, Castor (the burial place of Sir Robert Wingfield); Johnny and Serena Bute; Donna Chisholm; Anthony Crichton-Stuart for editorial comments and invaluable support; Sophie Crichton-Stuart; Edinburgh Central Library; Edinburgh University Library; Scott Fobister for many years of discussions on Mary Queen of Scots that began on our first visit to Craigmillar Castle; Antonia Fraser; Robin Harcourt-Williams, Librarian and Archivist for the Marquess of Salisbury at Hatfield House, for providing information on Robert Wingfield's letters in the Cecil Papers; Colin Henderson; Keith Hunter; Christine Irvine; Stephen Jenkins; Agnes Lyons; Dave McClay of the National Library of Scotland; Roisin MacDougall; Laura McShane; Mairi McVey; Lynsey Nairn for invaluable research assistance; Mike Page and all the staff of the Surrey History Centre; Heather Shanks for patiently proofreading the drafts; Tony Shorey; the Talbot Hotel, Oundle, for allowing me to take photographs of the Fotheringhay staircase; David Taylor of Blairs Museum; Alex Webster.

## Further reading

The literature on Mary Queen of Scots is vast. The following is a short list of works that have been especially useful in the preparation of this book.

Of all the general biographies available, there are two outstanding works currently in print, these being Antonia Fraser's much reprinted *Mary Queen of Scots* (London, 1969) and John Guy's *'My Heart is My Own': The Life of Mary Queen of Scots*, London, 2004. For discussions on contemporary literature concerning Mary and her execution, James Emerson Phillips, *Images of a Queen: Mary Stuart in Sixteenth Century Literature* (California, 1964) is a fascinating account, as are the more recent works of Jayne Elizabeth Lewis: *Mary Queen of Scots Romance and Nation* (London and New York, 1998) and *The Trial of Mary Queen of Scots. A Brief History with Documents* (Boston, 1999), although it is the view of the present writer that Lewis takes a too literary rather than a historical analysis of Wingfield's account of the execution and this should consequently be read with caution. For an analysis of the visual record of Mary's life, death and posthumous reputation, see Helen Smailes and Duncan Thomson, *The Queen's Image* (National Galleries of Scotland, Edinburgh, 1987). The final years of Mary's English captivity are admirably covered in Alan G.R. Smith (ed.), *The Last Years of Mary Queen of Scots: Documents from the Cecil Papers at Hatfield House* (Roxburgh Club, London, 1990). For the execution itself and additional printed versions of Wingfield's account see: William K. Boyd (ed.), *Calendar of State Papers Relating to Scotland and Mary, Queen of Scots 1547–1603* (Glasgow, 1915); Charles Dack, *The Trial, Execution and Death of Mary Queen of Scots*, Northampton and London, 1889; Henry Ellis, *Original Letters Illustrative of English History*, 2nd series, vol. III (London, 1827); The Hon. Mrs Maxwell-Scott, *The Tragedy of Fotheringay* (London, 1895); and A. Francis Steuart, *Trial of Mary Queen of Scots* (Edinburgh and London, 1923). For a short book on Robert Scarlett, the grave-digger of Peterborough, see George Dixon, *Old Scarlett* (privately printed, 1980; second edition, 1997). For Sir Robert Wingfield of Upton see Dack (as above), the relevant volumes of the series of twenty-four published by the Historical Manuscripts Commission, *Calendar of Manuscripts of the Most Hon. The Marquis of Salisbury Preserved at Hatfield House* (1883–1976), and his entry in P.W. Hasler (ed.), *The House of Commons 1558–1603. Vol. III. Members M–Z* (HMSO, 1981).

Coat of Arms of the Scottish Monarchy from a heraldic manuscript of c.1570.